What do you do when
you're COOPED UP at home;
when you're feeling stir-crazy
to get out and roam?

Build a fort with
a cushion,
a blanket
and sheet.

It's your place to get away;
your private retreat.

Perform a puppet show for your little brother.

Record it and send it to your great grandmother.

Work on a puzzle.
Go at your own pace.

You'll feel proud when you get
the last piece in it's place.

Bake a cake with your mom
for no reason at all.

We're in this together,
and for the long haul.

Gather the whole family
to play a board game.

Win or lose, you'll be joyful
and they'll feel the same.

Practice an instrument you already play.

Compose your own song called, "What I did Today".

Use drawings and art to express how you feel.

Paint imaginary pets or some that are real.

Keep up with your schoolwork,
and learn something new.

Chat online with a relative,
and classmates too.

Write letters to friends
you've not seen in a while.

Show them they are special,
and make them all smile.

Curl up with your family,
find a movie to watch.

Laughing together takes
family-time up a notch.

It's okay to miss normalcy, family and friends.

We'll appreciate our blessings much more when this ends.

www.ingramcontent.com/pod-product-compliance
Lightning Source LLC
Chambersburg PA
CBHW040117170426
42811CB00123B/1461